Published by
Lulu.Com

ISBN: 978-1-4357-1857-9

A GUIDE TO COLLEGE CHOICES FOR THE PERFORMING AND VISUAL ARTS

Kavin Buck
Edward Schoenberg

South LaBrea

"I would teach children music, physics and philosophy; but most importantly music, for in the patterns of music and all the arts are the keys of learning."

~ Plato, Philosopher

TABLE OF CONTENTS

Page 1	Introduction
Page 3	Arts Education and The Creative Economy
Page 5	College Types
Page 10	Degrees
Page 13	Finding the Right Fit
Page 16	Choosing a Major
Page 19	FAQ's
Page 22	Summer Programs
Page 24	Art School, Not Art Therapy
Page 26	The Audition and Portfolio
Page 27	Audition Guides for the Performing Arts
Page 28	*Acting / Theater*
Page 29	*Musical Theater*
Page 30	*Dance*
Page 31	*Music*
Page 32	Guidelines for the Visual Arts
Page 36	*Architecture*
Page 38	*Film / Cinema / Television*
Page 39	Web Resources
Page 48	Contact and Workshop Information
Page 57	Thanks

"The life of the arts is far from an interruption, a distraction, in the life of a nation, it is close to the center of a nation's purpose — and is a test of the quality of a nation's civilization."

~ John F. Kennedy, 35th U.S. President

INTRODUCTION

Art school is real college! The myth that an arts-based curriculum is easy is just that, a myth. In most undergraduate arts-based programs or institutions, with the exception of some trade/technical schools, students are required to complete course work in the liberal arts and science alongside their rigorous arts training. Students carry a full load of studio and academic course work while also having to make time for homework and their studio projects or practice sessions. Along with homework, many students must balance performance schedules, exhibition dates, internships or community service required for the artistic educational experience. The notion that students are free to create anything they want while attending art school because they are "artists" needs to be laid to rest. Art schools, university programs and conservatories have specific curriculum, direction and focus; while students can bring their own creative ideas into their course work, seldom do they get to "do their own thing" exclusively.

Once a student has decided he or she wants to pursue an arts education, finding the right performing or visual arts program to fit his or her artistic needs is a unique and individual decision. Each young artist will have his or her own methods of learning, ideas of what makes a school appealing or not, and extracurricular priorities and considerations. The art student's decision includes consideration of the differences between public and private colleges and universities, and encompasses large universities, small liberal arts colleges, conservatories, private art schools and trade/technical programs. Making a final decision to apply to any particular institution should take into consideration the student's artistic direction, the institution's location, financial situation, and short- and long-term goals.

Our intention with this publication is to objectively help students, parents and counselors start the process of preparing a "needs and wants" list, not to limit them by recommending a particular type of institution or style of education, or to rank individual programs.

"I know the price of success: dedication, hard work and an unremitting devotion to the things you want to see happen."

~ Frank Lloyd Wright, Architect

"The aim of art is to represent not the outward appearance of things but their inward significance."

~ Aristotle, Philosopher

ARTS EDUCATION AND THE CREATIVE ECONOMY

Often the biggest obstacle for a student who wishes to study the visual or performing arts is the parental and/or societal belief that a degree in art is not helpful in the marketplace. Fortunately for the students earning degrees in the arts, just the opposite is true. There have been a number of books and articles written in the past few years that have touted the "Creative Economy." Among these works are *"The Rise of the Creative Class"* by Richard Florida, Daniel Pink's *"The MFA is the New MBA"* in the Harvard Review, and the March 2000 Time Magazine article, *"The Redesigning of America."* In the Time article the author says,"Ladies and gentlemen, may we present the design economy. It is the crossroads where prosperity and technology meet culture and marketing." Most of what was forecast in this 2000 article has come to fruition in 2008. Not convinced? Just think iPod, Mini Cooper, "green" fashion, iPhones, and Wii Systems, to name a few. How a product looks and feels is as important as what it does. What a product does is determined by engineers and scientists; how it looks, sounds, and feels is determined by artists and designers. Another document worth reviewing was commissioned by Otis College of Art and Design and produced by the Los Angeles Economic Development Corporation (LAEDC), the *"Report on the Creative Economy of the L.A. Region."* Like the other works cited above, this document shows the importance of artists and designers to the current and emerging economies in one of the most vibrant regions in the U.S.

Ever stay after a movie and watch the credits or read the credits on the liner note of a compact disk? If you have, then you have seen people listed as digital artist, special effects designer, digital designer, animator, engineer, musician, etc. These are the kinds of fields for which the study of the arts is an excellent preparation. Check the U.S. Bureau of Labor Statistics forecast for future labor needs. You will find that there is an increasing need for artists and designers. It stands to reason that in today's marketplace, where rapid change is the norm and where art and technology integrate, the need for creative thinkers and collaborative problem solvers will continue to grow. Again, creativity and collaboration are cornerstones of most arts educations. For the performing artists the emergence of online entertainment outlets, indie music, indie film and dance companies all offer new avenues where performers can reach audiences and start careers.

Remember, students coming out of visual and performing arts programs not only have their degrees, they have sophisticated port-folios, reels, and electronic recordings of performances. All the afore-mentioned are designed to show, not tell, a future employer that the arts graduate is not only knowledgeable but also skilled and creative.

"Art is the only way to run away without leaving home."

~ Twyla Tharp, Dancer

"Art is for people who want to lead self-directed lives."

~ Suzanne Lacey, Artist/Educator

"Everything that is not in nature was designed by mankind."

~ Anonymous

COLLEGE TYPES

As with all college searches, students should begin the selection process as early as possible. Waiting until the last minute may result in the application, audition, or portfolio being less than perfect and/or lead to the wrong choice of program for the student's artistic needs.

There are many different types of schools offering an exceptional education in the arts. This chapter provides a list of four distinct categories that represent the majority of programs offered within the United States. By starting with these categories, students can begin to look at their choices and possibly narrow down their preferences based on type of institution. Each school is unique when it comes to size, curriculum, faculty, and facilities, so it is recommended that students research each option to obtain specific information regarding each distinctive program.

FOUR-YEAR COLLEGES AND UNIVERSITIES

Colleges and universities are good fits for students who wish both to major in the arts and experience a broad liberal arts and science background while participating in the full traditional collegiate experience.

For students looking for an arts education that also has a broad liberal arts curriculum, the university style of education may be the right fit. Universities require students to complete coursework in the liberal arts outside of their major field of study, typically in areas such as English, history, and the sciences. Non-art studies can and should inspire artistic practice, to initiate the possibility of a second major or cause them to reconsider their art focus. The ability to double major or switch majors is a useful safety net for those who aren't 100% certain of their choices. Some select universities have professional schools within their campuses that offer students conservatory or art school programs.

Four-year colleges and universities offer two individual approaches to arts-based education:

1. Arts majors that are embedded into the larger curriculum of the institution.
- *Primarily for students looking to continue their arts interest while pursuing a non-arts-based major.*
- *Generally less competitive when it comes to the arts.*
- *By and large do not require a portfolio or auditions for admissions.*
- *Classes commonly open to non-majors who have fulfilled the course prerequisites.*

2. Professional schools of art and conservatories as part of a larger college or university.
- *For the student who has a strong interest in engaging in the arts as a career.*
- *Generally admissions range from competitive to highly selective.*
- *Commonly use portfolios, auditions and supplemental materials as part of the admissions process.*
- *The majority of courses, specifically upper-division classes, are closed to non-majors.*
- *Offer small arts-based college or conservatory education with the advantages of a liberal arts college or research university.*

Examples:

Carnegie Mellon University	Temple University
Florida State University	UCLA
New York University	University of Hartford
Oberlin College	University of Michigan
Southern Methodist University	Virginia Commonwealth University
SUNY, Purchase	Yale University

FOUR-YEAR PERFORMING AND VISUAL ARTS SCHOOLS

Like universities, these schools generally offer art instruction couched in a liberal arts program of study, granting degrees at the Bachelor's and Master's levels. All degrees offered are art-related, and the required liberal arts coursework is more focused toward an arts perspective. Students who choose to attend art schools generally want a small-college atmosphere that will allow them to be surrounded by others who have a passion for the arts. Although liberal arts is incorporated in art school curriculum, students usually may not change majors outside the fields of visual or performing arts.

Examples:

Art Center College of Design
California College of the Arts
California Institute of the Arts
College for Creative Studies
Corcoran College of Art & Design
Cornish College of the Arts
Emily Carr Institute of Art
Fashion Institute of Technology
Kansas City Art Institute
Laguna College of Art & Design
Maryland Institute College of Art
Massachusetts College of Art and Design
Memphis College of Art
Minneapolis College of Art & Design
Nova Scotia College of Art & Design
Oregon College of Arts and Crafts
Otis College of Art & Design
Pacific Northwest College of Art
Parsons School of Design
Ringling College of Art
San Francisco Art Institute
School of the Art Institute of Chicago
School of the Museum of Fine Arts, Boston

CONSERVATORIES

Unlike universities or art schools, conservatories are professional schools designed to preserve and perfect the knowledge of the performing arts, in general without the traditional liberal arts curriculum. Conservatories commonly regard the arts as both an art form and a discipline, nurturing legacies of the past as well as offering contemporary issues and challenges. The majority of students who apply to conservatories self-select, or are recommended by instructors and/or professionals in the field. Predominantly, conservatories are looking for polish from a prospective student. Some conservatories are located within universities (see four-year colleges/universities, professional schools), while others are vocational institutions. Degrees differ from institution to institution and can range from offering the academic professional degrees, the artist diploma as a solely performance-based degree, and non-professional degrees such as Bachelor of Arts in Music Education.

Examples:

American Conservatory Theater
Berklee College of Music
Boston Conservatory
Cleveland Institute of Music
Colburn School of Music
Curtis Institute of Music
Juilliard School
Manhattan School of Music
Mannes College of Music
New England Conservatory of Music
Oberlin Conservatory of Music
San Francisco Conservatory of Music

VOCATIONAL/CAREER AND TECHNICAL SCHOOLS

A vocational/career and technical education prepares students for careers in particular arts-related fields. Coursework is practical and hands-on, giving a genuine feel for the tasks that will be pursued in a related line of work. The primary goal of such programs is to make students marketable in the workplace the day they graduate. This is the most employment-targeted education, and in recent years it has seen a boom with the growth of the film, graphic design, and internet/digital industry.

"Contemporary art challenges us... it broadens our horizons. It asks us to think beyond the limits of conventional wisdom."

~ Eli Broad, philanthropist and art collector

DEGREES

When choosing a place to study you will also want to find the degree that best fits both your short- and long-range plans. Different college and universities offer an array of options, with many giving multiple choices. All degrees mark or celebrate the completion of a particular program or major, but some do not allow you to continue on to more advanced degrees later.

ACCREDITATION

Accreditation is a type of quality-assurance process under which a facility's or institution's services and operations are examined by a third-party accrediting agency to determine if applicable standards are met. Should the school meet the accrediting agency's standards, the school receives accredited status from the accrediting agency. In the United States, educational accreditation is mostly performed by regional private nonprofit membership associations.

Despite the widely recognized benefits and accountability of accreditation, some institutions choose, for various reasons, not to participate in an accreditation process. It is possible for postsecondary educational institutions and programs to elect not to seek accreditation but nevertheless provide a quality postsecondary education. Yet other unaccredited schools simply award degrees and diploma without merit for a price.

An ongoing problem within higher education accreditation is the existence of diploma mills and accreditation mills. These organizations exist to grant apparent degrees without course work and give a willing buyer a degree for money. Sometimes both the buyer and seller know this, or sometimes a potential student is not aware of the fraud. In some cases a diploma mill and/or its "accreditor" is unrecognized and exists only at a post office box or Web page owned by the proprietor of the school. In the United States, unaccredited degrees may not be acceptable for financial aid, civil service, or other employment.

CERTIFICATES

Certificates are generally tied to the employment needs of a particular industry, local community or area employers. Usually offered through continuing education divisions, community colleges and some professional trade/technical colleges, they promote local economic development with non-credit courses and training programs that serve individuals, businesses, and organizations. Certificate program have seen large growth in recent years around the digital arts and through distance-learning programs.

AD (Artist Diploma)

An Artist Diploma is a non-academic degree that is solely based on the performance of the student's artistic practice.

BA (Bachelor of Arts)
50 - 60% coursework in liberal arts and sciences
40 - 50% coursework in the arts

A Bachelor of Arts degree is designed for students who are interested in a significant breadth of experience, not only in their art practice but also in the liberal arts and sciences. The BA degree places equal emphasis on academic studies and studio courses. Coursework in liberal arts serves to complement the arts major and integrates knowledge from a variety of disciplinary and/or interdisciplinary subjects. Students, for example, can choose to focus on their liberal arts studies or even double-major in such areas as psychology and education. The choice of an area of concentration is often associated with a student's post-graduation plans.

BFA (Bachelor of Fine Arts)
BM (Bachelor of Music)
30 - 35% coursework in liberal arts and sciences
65 - 70% coursework in the arts

A Bachelor of Fine Arts or Music degree is an initial professional degree and is designed to train graduates to be professional artists. The BFA or BM programs are for students who want to focus immediately on their specific artistic skills. If a student knows without a doubt that he or she wants to pursue a major in the arts, a quality BFA/ BM program may be the right choice. The majority of these programs at private colleges, conservatories, or universities require an audition or portfolio, even if a student has been admitted into the main school.

BArch (Bachelor of Architecture)
30 - 35% coursework in liberal arts and sciences
65 - 70% coursework in the arts

The Bachelor of Architecture degree usually requires full-time attendance for five years with an additional six months practical experience taken concurrently with program progress and prior to a Graduation Project. The Bachelor of Architecture degree may be awarded with Honors based upon the quality of performance in the program and current faculty regulations.

"No one can arrive from being talented alone, work transforms talent into genius."

~ Anna Pavlova, Dancer

"Ever tried. Ever failed. No matter. Try again. Fail again. Fail better."

~ Samuel Beckett, Playwright

FINDING THE RIGHT FIT

When seeking the right college fit, try making a "needs and wants" list. This could include the size of the school or program, type of facilities, location, reputation and/or selectivity; take time to look at every aspect of the institution.

ENROLLMENT

The number of students enrolled at a school can have an impact on the overall environment and atmosphere of the institution. A university with thousands of students will have a variety of extracurricular activities available to accommodate a broad range of interests. A private arts college or conservatory with a smaller student body may be less socially distracting.

In terms of students' studies, the student-to-faculty ratio is the important factor in school size. Often these ratios are smaller at the private schools. However, at the university the ratio generally improves as students' studies becomes more focused. While students are completing their general liberal arts coursework (history, sciences, etc.), students may be in lecture classes with more than 100 students, but the size of performing or visual arts courses may be as low as the private schools. The ratio will differ from college to college and from major to major. It is best to consult with each college's admissions office to get up-to-date information.

LOCATION

Location is an important factor in choosing a college. Stellar programs can be found in all parts of the country; they can be found in both large cities and rural communities and in the north, south, east, and west. The converse is also true, so it is important that when researching college choices students understand how location affects the college experience.

Depending on the type of career and education the student is looking for, there may be many factors to consider when choosing where to study. For the art student, these can include access to professional venues such as museums, galleries, theaters, and concert halls. Students may want to find out if these venues attract regional, national, or international talent that can inspire and educate them beyond the college classroom. Additionally, the opportunity to perform, exhibit, and find internships is vital to a young artist's education.

FACILITIES

Make sure the campus facilities meet the student's need for his or her artistic practice. Here are a few questions a student may ask a college representative:
- *What type of equipment do you have?*
- *Is it up to date? (This can include labs [photography, sculpture, etc.] as well as software and hardware).*
- *Is there adequate studio space and/or are there adequate practice rooms?*
- *Is there space available in the dorms to work?*
- *Are there multiple exhibition/performance spaces available to students?*
- *Is the campus "plugged in"?*
- *Does the library meet my needs?*
- *Do I have access to labs, classrooms, and practice facilities after hours?*

REPUTATION

Reputations far outlast reality. Students should not simply rely on recommendations and reputations, especially in the arts. It is always helpful to spend time checking the following information:

- *Are the instructors known in their field?*
- *Is the school respected in the industry?*
- *What created the school's reputation, and is it still valid?*
- *Even though the school is well known, is it right for me?*

Sometimes third-party information can be useful in helping discern an institution's reputation among people who work with and/or hire graduates of that school. Go to the web site of a company or organization for which you have respect that hires artists and designers and see where the artists and designers already working there earned their degrees. Also, organizations such as the Council of Fashion Designers of America (CFDA), the Donghia Foundation, and SIGGRAPH all sponsor scholarship competitions for college artists and designers, so looking at the schools that produced the winners of those scholarships could be helpful. Finally, ask working artists, designers and performing artists as well as art teachers in your area what they think about the schools you are considering.

ADMISSIONS CRITERIA

Each college has a different concept of its ideal student. Some institutions place greater value on academics, such as GPA, test scores, and writing, while others lean toward the student's portfolio or audition. Most colleges balance the student's creative talent with his or her academic achievements. Contact each school to find out its admissions requirements.

REMEMBER

Don't be afraid to ask a lot of questions; very few institutions will meet 100% of your wants. Make a pros and cons list for each school to compare with each other and to compare to your needs and wants.

"If a day goes by without my doing something related to photography, it's as though I've neglected something essential to my existence, as though I had forgotten to wake up."

~ Richard Avedon, Photographer

CHOOSING A MAJOR

Think globally! Thinking about a job in the arts is different from thinking about a career in the arts. An arts education is much more than just technical training.

When choosing a major, students should look beyond major's title and read a detailed description of the curriculum to make certain the program delivers what they seek and confers the degree they want. Colleges refer to their majors by different names as a way to market to different audiences. A student should look closely before deciding whether a major is a right or wrong fit.

Most undergraduate programs give students an array of curricular choices in each distinctive arts practice. This is to allow young artists to explore options and avenues in the arts that they may never have known existed prior to entering college. The ability to adapt, grow and move forward is important in today's work force and a necessity in the performing and visual arts. An expansive major gives students more choices as they continue to grow as artists after college.

"You don't choose to be an artist, art chooses you."

~ Anonymous

Many majors overlap with each other in specific areas. Be open to exploring all the available options that each college provides.

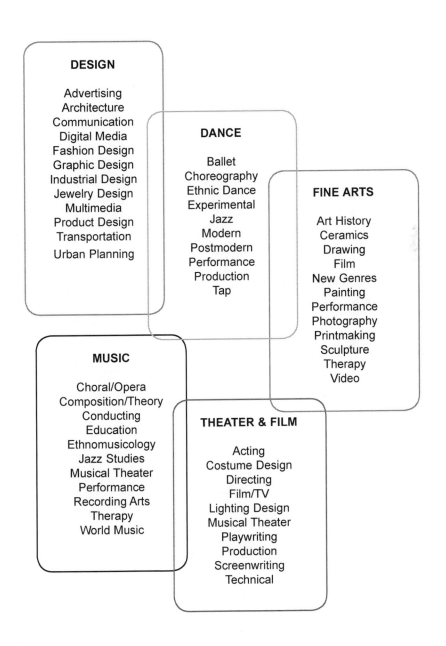

DESIGN

Advertising
Architecture
Communication
Digital Media
Fashion Design
Graphic Design
Industrial Design
Jewelry Design
Multimedia
Product Design
Transportation
Urban Planning

DANCE

Ballet
Choreography
Ethnic Dance
Experimental
Jazz
Modern
Postmodern
Performance
Production
Tap

FINE ARTS

Art History
Ceramics
Drawing
Film
New Genres
Painting
Performance
Photography
Printmaking
Sculpture
Therapy
Video

MUSIC

Choral/Opera
Composition/Theory
Conducting
Education
Ethnomusicology
Jazz Studies
Musical Theater
Performance
Recording Arts
Therapy
World Music

THEATER & FILM

Acting
Costume Design
Directing
Film/TV
Lighting Design
Musical Theater
Playwriting
Production
Screenwriting
Technical

"There comes a moment in a young artist's life when he knows he has to bring something to the stage from within himself. He has to put in something in order to be able to take something out."

~ Mikhail Baryshnikov, Dancer

"True art is characterized by an irresistible urge in the creative artist."

~ Albert Einstein

FAQ's

WHAT MAKES AN ART SCHOOL ENVIRONMENT DIFFERENT?

Students attending arts programs are generally expecting college venues where their art can be shown, expressed, and performed. They are looking for an environment where they can experience and participate in quality visual and performing arts activities. Art students look forward to the camaraderie of other artists, the interaction and exchange of ideas, and the healthy competition of other equally creative peers. Students who will be successful in a selective arts program should expect to concentrate and improve their art-making abilities both conceptually and technically while at college. They should look forward to the education and training that will prepare them to contribute artistically to their community and culture.

I"M NOT SURE OF MY COMMITMENT TO STUDYING ART. IS ART SCHOOL A RIGHT FIT FOR ME?

Students considering majoring in the arts should realize the professional and demanding nature of arts programs. Most institutions require a minimum of 15-20 hours of artistic work per week outside of the studio, laboratory or classroom. If students have a performance or gallery exhibition scheduled, those hours might and probably will increase. Administrators and faculty agree that higher education in the arts is not for the faint of heart, it is not for the procrastinator, those not interested in learning, or the person who mocks the adage "Creativity is 10% inspiration and 90% perspiration."

I DID WELL IN MY ART COURSES, BUT NOT AS WELL IN MY ACADEMIC COURSES. WILL I GET IN?

Professionally focused performing and/or visual art programs are not an alternative style of education. Most art colleges and universities weigh the academic and artistic ability of each student equally. Some put more emphasis on one aspect or the other, but the competitive student will show an equal balance of artistry and academic achievement. Many students falsely believe if they achieve high marks in visual and performing arts classes, and perform well in an audition or submit a strong portfolio, art schools will accept substandard grades in their academic courses. In most cases this is incorrect.

HOW DOES MY ART DEGREE APPLY TO THE REAL WORLD?

Students should understand that an education in the arts can and will prepare them for many different professions. Arts education is a primarily a critique-based style of education. Those who respond to tactile and visceral information can and do perform well. They may translate this style of learning to creative problem solving, strong intuitive reflex, initiative, self-motivation, confidence in self and in individual choices, and ability to work well with others. Each discipline is varied and offers many opportunities to excel both inside and outside of the arts community.

DOES AN ARTS-BASED DEGREE GUARANTEE I"LL FIND A JOB AFTER GRADUATION?

Confusing an arts-based education with trade and technical college is a common misconception. Call the English department, mathematics, geography, physics, or even medieval history departments of any college or university and you will get the same answer: "No, we do not guarantee employment upon graduation." If you survey a group of parents who have received a bachelor's degree, you will find that the vast majority will not be working within a profession in which they received their degree. Because of the growth in the design, internet, and entertainment industries, there is a myth that students should be able to land lucrative positions in the arts. Like graduates of all majors and professions, all but a very few graduates will have to work their way up to the top of their chosen arts discipline, and like graduates of all majors each artist will be able to choose many different directions to follow (including many outside the arts).

I'M INTERESTED IN GOING TO GRADUATE SCHOOL. DOES AN UNDERGRADUATE ART DEGREE PREPARE ME FOR GRADUATE SCHOOL?

Students worried about limiting their options by receiving a BA, BFA, or BM should not fret. All three are Baccalaureate degrees, and upon completion students can go on to receive advanced degrees. Entering specialized degree programs such as law and medical school may require some extra course work.

"One can have no smaller or greater mastery than the mastery of oneself."

~ Leonardo Da Vinci, Artist/Inventor

"Music is your own experience, your thoughts, your wisdom. If you don't live it, it won't come out of your horn."
~ Charlie Parker, Musician

SUMMER PROGRAMS

For students thinking about attending a visual or performing arts college, participating in a summer program is a good way to help build skills and expand a young artist's repertoire. It also allows students to explore whether or not an arts-based college education is the right kind of study for them, as well as assists them in preparation for competitive admissions processes.

There are several hundred programs world-wide that are available, with many of the college-sponsored programs designed specifically to mirror the "college experience." That is, the program's curriculum is a sample of what a student would get at that college. These programs are also good ways to network with faculty (who could be helpful with letters of recommendations when application time comes) and other students who have similar interests in the arts.

In performing arts programs young artists will get additional audition and performance experience that will be helpful when preparing for college auditions. Visual arts and design programs will provide students with additional studio experience and will help them build a body of work from which they can create part of their portfolio. In both cases students will have the opportunity not only to study and learn with new instructors, but also to participate in critiques with peers from outside their high school or local community. This interaction can give students a larger perspective on their performing or visual arts practice.

Most summer programs, institutes or workshops are rigorous and not aimed for students who are looking for a "summer camp" experience. Many programs, however, do include field trips to museums, galleries, studios, concert halls, and theaters. Some of the residential programs do have cultural, social, and recreational programming. However, it cannot be overemphasized that the main purpose of these programs is to prepare students for future study in the arts.

Age minimums for these programs can vary, but most start

at 15. Many students do two or three separate summer programs as a way of sampling different colleges in which they have interest. If students hope to apply their summer courses to a four-year institution they should remember that transferable college credit may or may not be granted at "pre-college" summer programs; it will depend on the program and the college to which the student applies. Students and parents should check with the programs for information on type of program (residential or day, etc.) costs, possibility of scholarships, conduct standards, and transferability of credit.

As with all educational choices, searching and selecting an appropriate summer program takes time. Make sure you research the program(s) carefully before making your selection.

"Practice what you know and it will help to make clear what you do not know."

~ *Rembrandt van Rijn, Artist*

ART SCHOOL, NOT ART THERAPY

There is a perception that art schools may provide students with a therapeutic environment. Nothing could be further from the truth. The Bachelor of Fine Arts or Bachelor of Music are professional degrees and are awarded at the end of a rigorous professional curriculum. Many university Bachelor of Arts degrees combine demanding arts training with highly competitive academic environments. Students participating in a performing or visual arts program are responsible for studio courses that require long hours inside and outside the classroom. They must also perform academically within their liberal arts classes in a private arts college or university setting. It is not unusual for these students to dedicate 50 to 60 hours per week working to meet the demands of classes, studio practice, and/or rehearsal time.

The use of performing and visual arts as part of a therapeutic process to treat and heal a wide range of emotional and psychological conditions has been successful in many different forms and practices. Parents often believe that if their child studies art in college it will provide a therapeutic environment. Parents may not realize that competitive performing and visual arts programs and their curricula are based on critique (read criticism) by faculty, fellow students, and outside artists, designers, and performers. Critique or critical analysis of a student's work is an important part of the art school experience. Students with fragile egos and/or emotional and psychological issues may be devastated by this part of the experience. In addition, the notion that students are free to create anything they want while attending art school because they are "artists" needs to be laid to rest. Art schools, university programs, and conservatories have specific curriculum, direction, and focus; while the students can bring their own creative ideas into their course work, seldom do they get to "do their own thing."

In conclusion, competitive art programs offer both a rigorous and demanding curriculum in which public criticism plays an important role in the educational process. The overall demands on students during the four years of undergraduate study are arduous and unquestionably not an alternative to professional art therapy.

**National Coalition of Creative Arts Therapies Associations
(NCCATA)**
www.nccata.org

**The American Art Therapy Association
(AATA)**
www.arttherapy.org

THE AUDITION AND PORTFOLIO

Making the choice to attend an arts program at a university, art school, or conservatory can be a tough decision for students and parents. Not only does the student have to go through the general academic admission requirements, there is also the added pressure of auditioning or submitting a portfolio. This extra effort is often the breaking point for many in the application process and it may even keep some from completing applications.

Most private art colleges or conservatories, and many selective public and private universities with professional schools or conservatories attached to them, require a portfolio review or audition for admission. Students considering higher education in the arts should be prepared for this requirement. Colleges request different procedures, so it is up to the student to contact his or her selected institutions as soon as possible to request portfolio or audition information. In many cases schools are looking for a demonstration of technical and conceptual skills. It is important to note that in most cases these reviews do not determine talent. They exist only to determine entrance to the college and placement in classes. Many students are devastated if denied entrance into a college of their choice. They interpret this as an indication of lack of talent. This is not how a denial should be interpreted. Typically, if students are denied it is because they are not prepared **at that time** to be successful in that particular program. More practice/work, more time invested, more commitment by the individual or outside instruction could turn an unfavorable decision into a favorable one.

The most important detail of preparing for an audition or portfolio submission is to allow ample time to rehearse and create the best work possible. It is virtually impossible to create quality work under a time constraint. Waiting until the last minute often dilutes the quality of the work or performance. Arts programs are highly competitive, and in many situations the audition or portfolio will be the deciding factor for the admissions committee.

AUDITION GUIDES FOR THE PERFORMING ARTS

The following guides are meant to assist students in preparing for general, not specific, auditions. The material provides students a starting point to prepare for auditions within the performing arts. Many individual majors have similar attributes when it comes to auditioning:

Punctuality - Arrive early and allow plenty of time before the audition to warm up and organize your thoughts. If a physical and vocal warm-up is not part of the audition, do so on your own.

Professionalism - Remember that the audition begins the minute you walk onto campus or into the building for off-site auditions.

Preparedness - Students should contact each university, school, or conservatory that requires an audition a year in advance to get its specific requirements.

THE ROLE OF THE PARENT

Unless the parent is the accompanist, his or her role during the audition should be minimal to non-existent. Parents should drop off their child, have lunch, or wait in the green room; parental anxiety affects the student, other auditioners, staff, and faculty.

ACTING / THEATER

Picture / Résumé
Bring a black and white or color 8" x 10" headshot and a résumé of credits, training and special skills (i.e., juggling, dance, acrobatics, stage combat, etc.) to the audition. For the photo, do not wear a hat or costume. Do not bring production shots from a show or film. The auditioner wants to see the student's face. Later the picture will help the auditioner recall the auditionee.

Monologue
Prepare two contrasting pieces: one contemporary and one Shakespearean or classical monologue. The number of audition pieces and the requirements will vary with each school. Check with the admissions office or department in advance regarding specific preferences. Most auditions are limited to two minutes per piece.

READ AND KNOW THE COMPLETE PLAY THAT INCORPORATES EACH MONOLOGUE. DO NOT USE STUDENT-WRITTEN MONOLOGUES.

What to Wear
Wear proper neutral-colored audition clothing that flatters the body and allows for easy movement. Most schools evaluate the actor's physicality as well as the content/emotion of the acting. Some schools have a physical "warm-up" as part of the audition process.

Recommendations
Bring at least one written letter of recommendation from an instructor or director.

Interview
Prepare for a personal interview about yourself. Be ready to articulate your immediate goals and your goals for the future. Understand the mission of the school for which you are auditioning, so that you may tell the interviewer how attending that particular school will help you achieve your goals.

MUSICAL THEATER

Picture / Résumé
As with the acting auditions, bring an 8" x 10" headshot and a résumé of credits to the audition. The photograph helps the director recall the student.

Representative Repertoire
Musical theater auditions include three areas of performance: acting, dancing and singing. The student should be strong in at least one of the three areas and satisfactory in the other two areas.

Acting - Prepare two contrasting monologues: one contemporary and one classical monologue. Requirements will vary with each school. Check with the admissions office or department in advance regarding specific requirements. (See "Acting" auditions.)

Dance - Group audition, combinations of ballet, jazz, tap and/or musical theater may be required. Often each dancer will be asked to perform the audition combination in a smaller group or solo.

Singing - Prepare at least 16 bars of two musical theater songs. One song should be up-tempo and the second song should be a ballad. The student should choose songs that are appropriate for his or her vocal range and character type. The student should be familiar with the musicals that feature the songs.

What to Wear
All students should wear comfortable, neutral-colored clothing that flatters the body. Dancers should bring extra dance clothes and shoes to change into or wear underneath outer clothing.

Note:
Although many colleges and universities offer musical theater as a major, often a musical theater program is located within the theater department or the music department.

DANCE

Choreography
Students should be prepared to take a master class with other auditioners and to perform an original dance solo. Choreography should be something the student has rehearsed and is comfortable performing. Although each school will have its own requirements, the piece is usually no more than 2-3 minutes in length.

What to Wear
Dancers should bring two clean, runless leotards and tights outfits. (The second outfit may be used as back-up in case of a mishap.)

WEAR DANCE CLOTHES THAT ARE COMFORTABLE AND FLATTERING BUT NOT TOO REVEALING. IT IS BETTER TO ERR ON THE CONSERVATIVE SIDE.

Shoes
Bring clean ballet, jazz, and character shoes. No street shoes.

Music
Bring two copies of pre-taped music for original choreography piece. Make sure the music is cued and ready to play.

Interview
Be prepared to discuss your original piece, especially when it is student choreographed. Know your immediate goals and your goals for the future. Understand the mission of the school for which you are auditioning so that you may articulate how attending that particular school will help you achieve your goals as a dancer.

Remember: Appearance and attitude do matter.

MUSIC

Representative Repertoire
Send a printed copy of your own repertoire with the music application and bring extra copies to the audition to hand to instructors.

Audition Pieces
Obtain the audition repertoire requirements well in advance. Each school will have its own requirements. Sometimes they are very specific. You should begin gathering this material from each school at least one year before your audition.

Recommendations
Include in your music application any additional recommendations from the primary instrument or vocal instructor with whom you have studied.

Sheet Music
Bring the original sheet music. Sometimes conservatories will not allow you to audition with photocopied materials. If you only have photocopied music, be sure it is organized in laminated plastic coverings and put in a binder for the audition.

Interview
Be prepared to discuss your previous training. Know your immediate goals and your goals for the future. Understand the mission of the school for which you are auditioning so that you may articulate how attending that particular school will help you achieve your goals as a musician.

GUIDELINES FOR
THE VISUAL ARTS

PORTFOLIO GUIDELINES

Unlike a face-to-face audition for the performing artist, a visual arts student's portfolio represents him or her to a college as a potential student and artist. For most university art programs and private art schools, the portfolio will be the main determining factor in the admissions process.

Editing the portfolio instead of building/creating a portfolio is the key to success in applying to competitive arts programs. Students should complete at least ten finished pieces for every one that is actually included in a final portfolio. Selecting what to include should not be a nerve-wracking experience. A young artist is usually his or her own worst critic and should follow the advice of the admissions counselors at the college regarding what to include in the portfolio. Students tend to edit pieces based on personal aesthetics and not on what the colleges seek. Admissions counselors are trained to know what exactly the admissions committee is looking for in a prospective student and can help edit a portfolio to meet the committee's requirements.

CATEGORIES

Most art programs want to see works that fall into three distinct categories: observational art, personal art, or a home exam. Some colleges require a combination of two or three categories, and others want to see only one category.

Observational Art
Observational art is drawing or painting in a traditional method using a still life, figure model, portrait, or landscape as the subject and rendering the subject as accurately as possible. The image should not

be taken from a photograph or the artist's imagination but from real life. Size of the artwork should be approximately 18" x 24" or larger in scale, and fill the entire surface of the paper or canvas. Most work in this category is done in pencil, charcoal, or other drawing media, but it can also include painting and collage.

Personal Art

Personal art is work done outside a classroom setting and reflects the artist's unique use of materials, subject matter and concept. Work can be completed in any medium including, but not limited to, drawing, painting, photography, mixed media, digital/computer art, film/video, ceramics, sculpture, animation, and performance art.

Home Exam

The home exam consists of specific work that has been required by a particular college or department. (Example: Rhode Island School of Design has traditionally asked for three drawings: The first drawing must represent a bicycle; the second, an interior or exterior environment; the subject matter for the third drawing is up to the applicant (the student may draw any object, subject, or situation).

Notes:

Photography submissions should be works that are shot and printed by the artist. When it comes to photography, schools are just as interested in why the student chose the subject as they are in how well it is printed.

PRESENTATION

Presentation of the portfolio is very important; consider it just like a personal interview. Due to the cost of mailing and lack of storage, most colleges will want the portfolio submitted in 35-mm slides or digital format. Original artwork, if requested, should be well documented prior to mailing in case the portfolio is lost or damaged in the mail. Follow each college's guidelines and if questions arise regarding submission of the portfolio don't hesitate to contact the admissions office of the school for specific directions.

TIPS

- *Always shoot and print enough images of each individual work so that you can send them to every school to which you are applying (it's better to have too many than too few). Always keep a master set you can duplicate at a later date if the originals get lost.*
- *If you are not comfortable photographing your own art, hire a professional. Many photo studios will photograph flat two-dimensional work for a fair price.*
- *Give yourself plenty of time prior to the portfolio due date. Documenting artwork can be tricky and it may take more than one attempt to get it right.*
- *For 35mm slides use a manual camera if possible.*
- *The background behind the artwork should be solid white or black depending upon the individual piece of art. DO NOT photograph artwork against a patterned wall, on a carpet or leaning against another object.*
- *Be sure to turn off the date and time signature on all digital cameras.*
- *When photographing indoors, use photoflood bulbs for lighting because a flash will often produce glare or hot spots.*
- *Outdoor photography usually produces even lighting. Be sure to prevent shadows from falling on two-dimensional work. Shadows are sometimes desirable for three-dimensional work if they help define edges or textures.*
- *Fill the frame in the viewfinder with the image of your work so that it is centered and parallel with the frame lines.*
- *If you still need to edit the image on 35mm slides, you can mask parts of the slide with a special tape that is sold in camera stores.*
- *Submit only focused and clear images.*
- *Label the 35mm slides with your name, date, title, and dimensions of the work. (Avery brand #5267 return-address labels work great for slides and can be printed on a home computer using most word-processing programs.)*
- *Include a separate typed slide description sheet.*

ORIGINAL ARTWORK

- Do not include torn or poorly cared-for work. Remember your portfolio is just like a personal interview; it represents you to the college or university.
- Only include your most recent work. Colleges are generally only interested in work done over the last year or two, the more recent the better. Showing eight to twelve pieces of art from the last six to twelve months demonstrates to the review committee that you produce work consistently.
- Include only finished or completed works (avoid sending too many studies or

gesture studies). Some schools will also want to see all or part of a sketchbook, but overall finished work shows the schools that you complete an idea from conception to conclusion.

- Include your name, date, and title of work on the back of each individual artwork.
- Photograph all three-dimensional/sculptural work (do not mail original three dimensional work).

ELECTRONIC PORTFOLIOS

Many colleges and university visual arts programs request electronic portfolios. The majority of these schools offer technology-based specializations such as graphic design, media arts, animation, architecture, etc. Do not assume the college will accept an electronic/new-media portfolio. Check with each college to see if it will accept new-media presentations and what format/programs it can accommodate. Videotapes or DVD's should not exceed the time limit imposed by the school and be cued to the start of any project. Make sure to identify either NTSC (North America format) or PAL (European format) on VHS tapes. If a college accepts websites, give the URL address that will direct the review committee to the first page you want them to see. Make sure it downloads fast and that all connecting links (music, video, text) work.

Some institutions also use services that allow students to upload their portfolios via the internet. This is the safest and most efficient way to submit your work to a college. There may be a small service charge to the student if the college is using a third-party vendor like Slideshow.com.

ARCHITECTURE

Architects take into account the building as a whole. They understand that architecture is an art form serving a larger objective of technology, materials, techniques, and innovation. It is a business with client responsibility.

The architect's role is one of constant inventiveness. For more intimate projects an architect can pilot a project from start to finish. For larger ventures that are more complex, the architect may become a leader of a team that will include many people at different stages, but as the creative force the architect will always be involved from the beginning to the end of the project.

Who is likely to choose Architecture?

Having a background in English and art (technical drawing, design, and technology) or science and math is helpful. The architect is the one person whose professional responsibility is to consider the building as a whole. This program is likely to be of interest to students who see themselves as:

- *Having good communication skills and the ability to work within a team and to a budget.*
- *Designing for a purpose and contributing in a positive way to the environment and to society.*
- *Using resources, materials, and technologies responsibly.*
- *Providing a positive, healthy environment internally and externally, and having a cultural significance that links it to its time and place and the extraordinarily rich history of architecture.*

Sample of advanced degrees in architecture:

Degree	Average Length	Academic Background
MArch I First professional degree program in architecture.	3 Years	AB, BA, BS (including four-year BA or BS in Architecture) Non-architecture undergraduate degree or four-year nonprofessional degree in architecture.
MArch II Second professional degree program in architecture.	2 Years	BArch (Five-year degree) Professional five-year undergraduate degree in architecture or foreign equivalent.
MA Academic degree in architecture oriented toward research and teaching.	2 Years	AB, BA, BS, or BArch Architecture or non-architecture undergraduate or graduate degree.
PhD Advanced academic program in architecture oriented toward research and teaching.	6 Years	AB, BA, BS, or BArch, Architecture MA, or MArch Architecture or non-architecture undergraduate or graduate degree.

FILM / CINEMA / TELEVISION

Résumé
A résumé of projects, credits and awards for creative work, including film projects, is recommended. Although many programs do not
require previous film experience, it is a good idea to list all production
experience on a résumé.

Writing Samples
Film and Television programs may require one or more of the following
writing samples in their portfolios:

- *Personal essay*
- *Critical essay on a film*
- *Dramatic or comedic essay*
- *Character profile*
- *Screenplay or theatrical play sample (approximately six pages)*

Film/Video Samples on DVD
Schools may require a produced live-action or animation film of approximately 10 minutes. The quality of the film is slightly less important than the content or creative ideas behind the film. Prepare and
edit these materials well in advance of their due date. DO NOT WAIT
UNTIL THE LAST MINUTE TO CREATE A FILM PROJECT.

Interview
In addition to the portfolio, an interview may also be included in the application process. Punctuality and appropriate attire are recommended for the interview. The interview is an opportunity to communicate
your educational and career goals to the faculty and ask questions
about the program.

Letters of Recommendation
Many programs require letters of recommendation (1-3) in their portfolios. They can be from an instructor, an employer, or anyone who
knows the student's work in film or another creative medium.

WEB RESOURCES

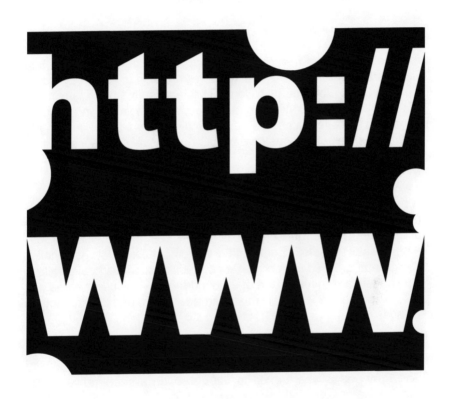

Academy of Film Schools
www.rivalquest.com/schools/
Film and media departments, programs and labs: around the world.

ArtLex.com - Visual Arts Dictionary
www.artlex.com
A free visual arts dictionary for artists, students, and educators in art production, criticism, history, aesthetics, and education. ArtLex has more that 3,300 terms, along with thousands of images, pronunciation notes, quotations, and links to other resources on the web.

ArtSchools.com
www.artschools.com
Artschools.com is a free college search engine that lists over 1,300 visual arts programs worldwide. Students are able to search by major, zip code, state, or type of college. The results list brief descriptions of the colleges with contact numbers and website links. On the home page, the site offers a number of instructive essays about applying to college, as well as various career opportunities within the visual arts.

Arts Deadlines List
www.xensei.com/users/adl
A monthly newsletter (via email or paper) with 600-900 announce-ments (every month!) listing art contests and competitions, art schol-arships and grants, juried exhibitions, art jobs and internships, call for entries/proposals/papers, writing and photo contests, residencies, design and architecture competitions, auditions, casting calls, fellow-ships, festivals, funding, and other opportunities (including some that take place on the web) for artists, art educators, and art students of all ages.

Arts Education Partnership
http://aep-arts.org
The Partnership was formed in 1995 through a cooperative agree-ment between the National Endowment for the Arts (NEA) and the United States Department of Education (USED) and is managed by the National Assembly of State Arts Agencies (NASAA) and the Council of Chief State School Officers (CCSSO). It is designed to demonstrate and promote the essential role of arts education in enabling all students to succeed in school, life, and work. Partners

include the following: arts, education, business, philanthropic and government organizations that have national scope, and state and local partnerships that promote educational policies supporting arts education.

Association for the Advancement of Arts Education (AAAE)

www.aaae.org
The AAAE is the direct result of a comprehensive two-year study that surveyed hundreds of superintendents, principals, teachers, parents, school board members, artists, professional arts administrators, and community leaders regarding their views on arts education.

Association of Independent Colleges of Art and Design (AICAD)

www.aicad.org
AICAD operates programs that inform the public about art and design colleges and programs that improve the quality of the member colleges. AICAD's 35 members are fully accredited, degree and diploma granting, free-standing colleges of art and design.

College Art Association (CAA)

www.collegeart.org
CAA includes among its members those who by vocation or avocation are concerned about and/or committed to the practice of art, including teaching and research of and about the visual arts and humanities. Over 13,000 artists, art historians, scholars, curators, collectors, educators, art publishers and other visual arts professionals are individual members. Another 2,000 university art and art history departments, museums, libraries, and professional and commercial organizations hold institutional memberships.

CollegeNET

www.collegenet.com
Launched in 1995, not a diskette, CD, or download system, CollegeNET lets applicants complete, file, and pay for their admissions applications entirely through the internet. Over 500 colleges and universities including Virginia Tech, Ohio State, and University of Washington have contracted with CollegeNET to serve as their official web-based admissions application. CollegeNET is a commercially sponsored college-oriented website that DOES NOT collect student data for sale to third parties.

Dance-Teacher.com
www.dance-teacher.com
Lifestyle Ventures, LLC, is the publisher of American Cheerleader®, Dance Spirit®, Dance Teacher®, Pointe®, In Motion® and Stage Directions® magazines, each of which is prepared and produced for a particular group of readers with special interests. American Cheerleader is the only national magazine written for the more than 3.3 million young people involved in cheerleading throughout the United States. Dance Spirit magazine is read by more young dancers and their teachers than any other dance publication. Dance Teacher, published for more than 20 years, is the only nationwide magazine addressed to dance teachers of all disciplines. Pointe magazine, the newest member of the group, published its debut issue in February 2000. It is an international ballet magazine for ballet dancers and serious ballet students. Stage Directions, now in its eleventh year, serves the strategic, practical, and technical information needs of small theaters across the country.

Enrichment Alley
www.enrichmentalley.com
Enrichment Alley was designed to enable students, families, schools, and advisors to find programs to enhance learning.

Filmmaker.com Library of Annotated Film Schools
www.filmmaker.com/reviews.html
If you're thinking of going to film school, you need an insider's opinion on going to film school. The Library of Annotated Film Schools (LOAFS) not only provides a comprehensive listing of film schools' websites from around the world, it also offers something that the film schools themselves do not reveal: honest, telling reviews and shared experiences from the film students themselves.

Film School Confidential
www.lather.com/fsc/intro.html
This book contains objective and subjective information about schools that offer M.F.A. degrees in film production. The objective information was obtained from the admissions offices of the schools discussed. The subjective information comes from interviews with students, graduates, and faculty from these schools.

GradSchools.com

www.gradschools.com

Gradschools.com is a free college search engine that lists over 50,000 graduate and professional degree programs.

International Network of Performing and Visual Arts Schools

www.artsschoolsnetwork.org

The International Network of Performing and Visual Arts Schools strives to inspire excellence in arts education. The Network supports and serves the leaders of specialized arts schools, fosters communication, promotes the development of new schools of the arts and provides leadership and direction in arts education.

London Association of Art & Design Education

www.laade.org

LAADE is a Visual Arts in Education organization representing London's art-education community.

Mariachi USA Foundation

www.mariachiusa.org

The Mariachi USA Foundation has benefited elementary and high school children by providing grants to promote folkloric music programs.

Music School Search

www.musicschoolsearch.com

Music School Search is also designed to help students make a music school choice.

Music Teachers National Association (MTNA)

www.mtna.org

Since 1876, Music Teachers National Association has existed to support music teaching and the art of music. Founded by Theodore Presser and 62 colleagues, MTNA is America's oldest professional music association. Today, MTNA is a non-profit organization of 24,000 independent and collegiate music teachers committed to furthering the art of music through programs that encourage and support teaching, performance, composition, and scholarly research.

Musical Theatre International (MTI)

www.mtishows.com

MTI is particularly dedicated to the idea of theater as education. Whether it's the 12,000 high schools who regularly perform in its shows or the many community and professional theaters whose outreach programs introduce new audiences to new works. MTI shares with these educators the goal of raising the next generation of theater artists and audiences.

National Alliance for Musical Theatre

http://www.namt.net

Membership is open to organizations that have been incorporated for a minimum of two years and that are involved in the presentation, production, and/or booking of musical theater performances. In special instances, exceptions are made for individuals who are independent producers.

National Art Educators Association (NAEA)

www.naea-reston.org

The NAEA was formed to promote art education through professional development, service, advancement of knowledge, and leadership. NAEA is a non-profit educational organization. Founded in 1947 with the merger of the Western, Pacific, Southeastern, and Eastern Region Art Associations, plus the art department of the National Education Association (NEA). NAEA has over 17,000 art educators from every level of instruction: early childhood, elementary, intermediate, secondary, college and university, administration, museum education. Members are from all 50 states plus the District of Columbia, U.S. Possessions, most Canadian Provinces, U.S. military bases around the world, and 25 foreign countries.

National Foundation for Advancement in the Arts (NFAA)

www.nfaa.org

High school seniors and other 17- and 18-year-old artists are eligible to apply to the NFAA's Arts Recognition and Talent Search (ARTS) program. Simply applying provides the opportunity to qualify for $3 million in college scholarships, share in an award package valued up to $800,000, and be named a Presidential Scholar in the Arts. Almost 10% of all the ARTS program applicants receive some kind of award or recognition for their talent. The ARTS program, one of several NFAA programs available to artists developing their careers, identifies promising 17- and 18-year-old artists in the categories of Dance, Jazz, Film and Video, Music, Photography, Theater, Visual Arts and Voice, and provides scholarships and financial support toward their continued arts education.

National Portfolio Day Association (NPDA)
www.npda.org
The National Portfolio Day Association hosts National Portfolio Day events throughout the United States and Canada. 97% of the participating colleges at NPDA events are private four-year accredited art schools. National Portfolio Days support the exchange of information about the student's work, and about the student and his or her college plans. No admissions decisions or scholarship awards will be offered to students at a National Portfolio Day.

Penrose Press International Directory
www.penrose-press.com/IDD
This site has links to colleges, universities, societies, conferences, and journals dealing with all types of art and design. Organized by country (in Chinese, English, French, German, Italian, and Spanish).

Performing and Visual Arts College Fairs
National Association for College Admission Counseling (NACAC)
www.nacacnet.org
NACAC Performing and Visual Arts College Fairs (PVAC Fairs) are events for college and college-bound students interested in pursuing undergraduate and graduate programs in the areas of visual arts, music, dance, theater and other related disciplines. Attendees learn about educational opportunities, admissions and financial aid, portfolio requirements, etc., by meeting with representatives from colleges, universities, and conservatories with specialized programs in the visual and performing arts.

Peterson's Guide to the Visual & Performing Arts
http://www.petersons.com/vpa/vpsector.html
Since 1966, Peterson's has helped to connect individuals and educational institutions with information about colleges and universities,

career schools, graduate programs, summer opportunities, study abroad, financial aid, test preparation, and career exploration.

Unified Application for Conservatory Admission

www.unifiedapps.org

The goal of admissions professionals and educators is to aid in the academic and artistic training of students. In an effort to allow students to devote more time to their education, nine premier conservatories have developed the Unified Application for Conservatory Admission, which may be used either for undergraduate or graduate admission.

Vocational/Technical College Search

www.collegelookup.com

CollegeLookup.com is a one-stop source for career training needs. Whether it's computers and technology, interior design, or the culinary arts, it is all at CollegeLookup.com. All the top career fields, from all the top schools.

Xap

www.xap.com

Xap is the pioneer in electronic and Internet-based information-management systems for college-bound students. It is the fastest growing internet company serving the higher education marketplace. Xap is the first company to partner directly with associations and institutions of higher learning to develop regional, university-approved Mentor™ websites. A Mentor™ site, as its name connotes, utilizes the internet to guide students efficiently through the comparison, selection, and application process of admission and financial aid. Xap's mission is to be the leader in building and providing students and their families, universities and sponsors the most comprehensive and widely used online information services for higher education.

National Association for College Admission Counseling

www.nacacnet.org

The National Association for College Admission Counseling (NACAC), founded in 1937, is an organization of more than 10,000 professionals from around the world dedicated to serving students as they make choices about pursuing postsecondary education.

State and Regional Associations

NACAC has 23 chartered state and regional affiliate associations that work to respond to the professional needs of their members and to be part of the delivery system for NACAC programs and services at the local level.

State and Regional Association Websites:

Dakota ACAC
www.dacac.com

Great Plains ACAC
www.gpacac.net

Hawaii ACAC
http://hacac.hawaii.edu

Illinios ACAC
www.iacac.org

Indiana ACAC
www.iacac.net

Iowa ACAC
www.iowaacac.org

Kentucky ACAC
www.kascac.com

Michigan ACAC
www.macac.org

Minnesota ACAC
www.mn-acac.org

Missouri ACAC
www.moacac.org

New England ACAC
www.iacac.org

New Jersey ACAC
www.njacac.com

New York ACAC
www.nysacac.org

Ohio ACAC
www.oacac.org

Overseas ACAC
www.oacac.com

Pacific Northwest ACAC
www.pnacac.org

Pennsylvania ACAC
www.pacac.org

Potomic and Chesapeake ACAC
www.pcacac.org

Rocky Mountain ACAC
www.rmacac.org

Southern ACAC
www.sacac.org

Texas ACAC
www.tacac.org

Western ACAC
www.wacac.org

Wisconsin ACAC
www.wacac.com

CONTACT AND WORKSHOP INFORMATION

For information regarding including a seminar or workshop based on this book at your conference, college fair, high school, community college, or special event, please contact:

southlabrea@yahoo.com

Contents for this publication compiled from previous lectures, seminars, courses and pre-conference workshops for NACAC and other state and regional parent associations as well as UCLA Extension, high schools, and community colleges.

PRESENTATIONS

National Association of College Admissions Counseling (NACAC)
2008
- Seattle, WA
2007
- Austin, TX
2006
- Pittsburgh, PA
2004
- Milwaukee, WI
2003
- Long Beach, CA
- Greater Los Angeles National College Fair
2002
- Salt Lake City, UT
- Greater Los Angeles National College Fair
2001
- Greater Los Angeles National College Fair
2000
- Washington, DC

Western Association of College Admissions Counseling (WACAC)
2008
- Flamingo Hotel and Resort, Las Vegas, NV
2007
- University of San Diego, CA
2006
- San Jose State University, CA
2005
- Soka University, Aliso Viejo, CA
- Share the Best, Mount Saint Mary's College, CA
2004
- Sonoma State University, Rohnert Park, CA
- Share the Best, University of San Diego, CA
- Share the Best, Mount Saint Mary's College, CA
2003
- Loyola Marymount University, Los Angeles, CA
- Share the Best, University of La Verne, CA

2002
- Share the Best, Mount Saint Mary's College, CA
- University of the Pacific, Stockton, CA

2001
- Occidental College, Los Angeles, CA

2000
- Chapman College, Chapman, CA

1999
- Saint Mary's College, Moraga, CA

Hawaii Association of College Admissions Counseling (HACAC)
2005
- Honolulu, HI

2003
- Honolulu, HI

2002
- Honolulu, HI
-

Rocky Mountain Association of College Admissions Counseling (RMACAC)
2008
- Tucson, AZ

Individual Workshops/Seminars
2008
- Wildwood School, Culver City, CA

2007
- El Camino Community College, Torrance, CA
- Oaks Christian High School, Westlake Village, CA
- Las Vegas Portfolio Day, Las Vegas, NV
- UCLA Extension, Los Angeles, CA
- Wildwood School, Culver City, CA
- Notre Dame High School, Sherman Oaks, CA

2006
- Truckee Meadows Community College, Reno, NV
- UCLA Extension, Los Angeles, CA (July & October)
- Las Vegas Portfolio Day, Las Vegas, NV

2005
- Truckee Meadows Community College, Reno, NV

- UCLA Extension, Los Angeles, CA
- Las Vegas Academy/Clark County School District, Las Vegas, NV
- Oaks Christian High School, Westlake Village, CA

2004
- UCLA Extension, Los Angeles, CA (April & November)

"I can't understand why people are frightened of new ideas. I'm frightened of the old ones."

~ John Cage, Composer

NOTES

NOTES

"Art is not the application of a canon of beauty but what the instinct and the brain can conceive beyond any canon."

~ Pablo Picasso, Artist

THANKS AND APPRECIATIONS

Kavin Buck
For my mom and dad (who did not come from an arts background), for their unconditional support of my attending art school. Also to Laura and Isabella for giving me inspiration both in and out of the studio.

Mr. Schoenberg wishes to thank the teachers who encouraged his interest in the performing arts. He also thanks his wife Marna for her support and his children, Jessica and Daniel, who are pursuing their passion for the visual and performing arts.

Mr. Buck and Mr. Schoenberg also wish to thank:

Jane Buckman
Tim Ford
Carol Kim
Alice Kleeman
Marc Meredith
Anthony Padilla
Mike Rivas
Yvette Sobky
Jenny Woo-Umhofer
Ken Young
Laura Young

And all the high school, community college counselors, college admissions professionals counselors, and educators who keep sending us articles, suggestions, and needs — keep them coming!

"Retire to what?"

~ Duke Ellington, Musician/Conductor

ABOUT THE AUTHORS

Kavin Buck has been a nationally exhibiting visual artist for over 20 years and is currently the Director of Enrollment Management and Outreach for the School of the Arts and Architecture at UCLA and adjunct faculty at Santa Monica College's Art Mentorship Program. He received his BFA from Otis College of Art and Design, and MFA from California Institute of the Arts, and completed post-graduate work with the Whitney Museum of American Art Independent Study Program in New York. In 1990 Mr. Buck received a PS-1 Museum Studies grant and has served both on the executive board and as president of the Western Association for College Admission Counseling.

Ed Schoenberg has a background in music and theater. He is the Vice President for Enrollment Management at Otis College of Art and Design in Los Angeles, California. He has served in admissions, financial aid, student affairs, and enrollment-management positions at nationally recognized liberal arts colleges, a state-supported research university, and comprehensive universities over the past 34 years. He received his BA from Whittier College and his MA in Counseling and Educational Psychology from the University of Nevada, Reno.

Made in the USA
San Bernardino, CA
30 March 2013